Crickets

by Cheryl Coughlan

Consulting Editor: Gail Saunders-Smith, Ph.D.

Consultant: Gary A. Dunn, Director of Education,
Young Entomologists' Society

Pebble Books

an imprint of Capstone Press
Mankato, Minnesota

Pebble Books are published by Capstone Press,
1710 Roe Crest Drive, North Mankato, Minnesota 56003
www.capstonepub.com

Library of Congress Cataloging-in-Publication Data
Coughlan, Cheryl.
    Crickets / by Cheryl Coughlan.
    p. cm.—(Insects)
    Includes bibliography and index.
    Summary: Simple text and photographs describe the physical characteristics
and habits of crickets.
      ISBN-13: 978-0-7368-0237-6 (hardcover) ISBN-13: 978-0-7368-8208-8 (paperback)
      ISBN-10: 0-7368-0237-1 (hardcover)   ISBN-10: 0-7368-8208-1 (paperback)
      1. Crickets—Juvenile literature. [1. Crickets.] I. Title. II. Series: Insects
(Mankato, Minn.)
Ql508.G8C68 1999
595.7′26—dc21

                                                  98-51626
                                                      CIP
                                                      AC

Note to Parents and Teachers

The Insects series supports national science standards for units on
the diversity and unity of life. The series shows that animals have
features that help them live in different environments. This book
describes and illustrates the parts of crickets. The photographs
support early readers in understanding the text. The repetition of
words and phrases helps early readers learn new words. This book
also introduces early readers to subject-specific vocabulary words,
which are defined in the Words to Know section. Early readers may
need assistance to read some words and to use the Table of
Contents, Words to Know, Read More, Internet Sites, and
Index/Word List sections of the book.

Printed in the United States of America in North Mankato, Minnesota.
042012   006691R

Table of Contents

4

Most crickets are
black or brown.

Some crickets live
on the ground.

8

Some crickets live
in trees.

antennas

Crickets have
two long antennas.

legs

Crickets have
two long legs.

legs

legs

Crickets have
four short legs.

ears

Crickets have ears
on their front legs.

wings

Most crickets have wings.

Many crickets chirp
at night.

Words to Know

antenna—a feeler on an insect's head

chirp—a sound a cricket makes; crickets chirp by rubbing together their two front wings; crickets chirp faster in warmer weather.

ear—a body part used for hearing; crickets have ear membranes on their front legs.

wing—a movable part of an insect that helps it fly; most crickets have four wings.

Read More

Berger, Melvin. *Chirping Crickets.* Let's-Read-and-Find-Out-Science. New York: HarperCollins, 1998.

Kranking, Kathy. *The Bug Book.* New York: Golden Books, 1998.

Ross, Michael Elsohn. *Cricketology.* Backyard Buddies. Minneapolis: Carolrhoda Books, 1996.

Internet Sites

FactHound offers a safe, fun way to find Internet sites related to this book. All of the sites on FactHound have been researched by our staff.

Here's how:

1. Visit *www.facthound.com*

2. Type in this special code **0736802371** for age-appropriate sites. Or enter a search word related to this book for a more general search.

3. Click on the **Fetch It** button.

FactHound will fetch the best sites for you!

Index/Word List

antennas, 11
black, 5
brown, 5
chirp, 21
crickets, 5, 7, 9, 11,
   13, 15, 17, 19, 21
ears, 17

front, 17
legs, 13, 15, 17
long, 11, 13
night, 21
short, 15
two, 11
wings, 19

Word Count: 48
Early-Intervention Level: 6

Editorial Credits
Mari C. Schuh, editor; Timothy Halldin, cover designer and illustrator;
   Kimberly Danger, photo researcher

Photo Credits
Bill Beatty, 16
Bill Johnson, 6
David Liebman, cover
Dembinsky Photo Assoc. Inc./Skip Moody, 10
Dwight R. Kuhn, 1
Frederick D. Atwood, 20
Rob Curtis, 12, 14, 18
Root Resources/Earl L. Kubis, 4
Visuals Unlimited/Joe McDonald, 8